Related by adoption

A handbook for grandparents and other relatives

Hedi Argent

with contributions from Kate Cairns
and Joyce and Eric Stanway

BAAF

OPTION
STERING

Published by
British Association for Adoption & Fostering
(BAAF)
Saffron House
6–10 Kirby Street
London EC1N 8TS
www.baaf.org.uk

Charity registration 275689 (England and Wales)
and SCO39337 (Scotland)

© Hedi Argent, 2004
Reprinted 2008, 2009, 2010
New edition 2011
Reprinted 2012

British Library Cataloguing in Publication Data
A catalogue record for this book is available from
the British Library

ISBN 978 1 907585 38 8

Project management by Shaila Shah,
Director of Publications, BAAF
Photographs on cover and in book posed by
models (except on p.57).
Designed by Andrew Haig & Associates
Typeset by Fravashi Aga
Printed in Great Britain by T J International
Trade distribution by Turnaround Publisher
Services, Unit 3, Olympia Trading Estate,
Coburg Road, London N22 6TZ

BAAF is the leading UK-wide membership
organisation for all those concerned with
adoption, fostering and child care issues.

MIX
Paper from
responsible sources
FSC® C013056

Contents

Introduction   1

1   What exactly is adoption?   6
2   The adoption process   8
3   Some legal points   20
4   Who are the children?   22
5   Family systems and circles   26
6   Continuity, connection and contact   31
7   Ethnicity, religion and culture   36
8   Common problems, questions and
    some answers   40
9   A tale of two generations of grandparents   57
10 Endpiece: What you can do   64

Useful organisations   67

Suggestions for further reading   70

Acknowledgements

I am grateful to Daphne Batty, Jeffrey Coleman, and Phillida Sawbridge for their helpful comments on successive drafts of this handbook. I also want to thank Shaila Shah, Director of Publications at BAAF, and her assistant, Jo Francis, for their unfailing patience and support. Finally, I am most indebted to all the adopters, grandparents and other relatives who have so generously shared their stories and whose voices can be heard throughout this book.

Hedi Argent
January 2004

This edition

This second edition of *Related by Adoption* has been comprehensively revised and updated in line with recent legislative changes.

Notes about the authors

Hedi Argent is an independent family placement consultant, trainer and freelance writer. She is the author of *Find me a Family* (Souvenir Press, 1984), *Whatever Happened to Adam?* (BAAF, 1998), *Related by Adoption* (BAAF, 2004), *One of the Family* (BAAF, 2005), *Ten Top Tips for Placing Children in Permanent Families* (BAAF, 2006), *Josh and Jaz have Three Mums* (BAAF, 2007), *Ten Top Tips for Placing Siblings* (BAAF, 2008), and Te*n Top Tips for Supporting Kinship Placements* (BAAF, 2009). She is the co-author of *Taking Extra Care* (BAAF, 1997, with Ailee Kerrane) and *Dealing with Disruption* (BAAF, 2006, with Jeffrey Coleman), and the editor of *Keeping the Doors Open* (BAAF, 1988), *See You Soon* (BAAF, 1995), *Staying Connected* (BAAF, 2002), and *Models of Adoption Support* (BAAF, 2003). She has also written six illustrated booklets in the children's series published by BAAF: *What Happens in Court?* (2003, with Mary Lane), *What is Contact?* (2004), *What is a Disability?* (2004), *Life Story Work* (2005, with Shaila Shah), *What is Kinship Care?* (2007) and *Adopting a Brother or Sister* (2010).

Kate Cairns is a social worker and teacher. She is also the author of *Surviving Paedophilia* (Treatham Books, 1999) and *Attachment, Trauma and Resilience* (BAAF, 2001), as well as several articles, and the co-author of *Learn the Child* (BAAF, 2004), *Safer Caring* (BAAF, 2007), *Transitions and Endings* (BAAF, 2008), and *Building Identity* (BAAF, 2008). Joyce and Eric Stanway are her parents.

Introduction

I do think children need a family and that's more than just a mum or a mum and dad. Jean's adopted children have got me and Auntie Mary and a granddad and their uncle and his wife – that's another auntie – and a cousin who lives further away with her family.
Grandparent of five adopted children

Adoption is a good way of building a family but it is different from having children born into the family. For grandparents there can be no poignant rush of familiarity – the child will not have your daughter's eyes or your son's habit of wrinkling his nose. Some of the joy of grandparenthood lies in the evident continuity of the generations. Some of the satisfaction of belonging to an extended family lies in the recognition that aunts and uncles and cousins have similarities that demonstrate the enduring nature of the family. But the adopted child comes from another line and adoption is proof that not all families endure.

One out of every three of us is, or will be, a grandparent. Approximately one out of every 75 people in the UK is adopted. This means that a very large number of people are grandparents to children who have been adopted.

Adoption today

At the beginning of the 21st century we see and hear a great deal about adoption in the newspapers and on television. Adoption is encouraged by government and pursued by all local authorities and voluntary agencies as the most permanent solution for children in the care system who cannot return to live with their birth families. Adoption by step-parents and adoption of children from overseas adds to the number of adopted young people in Britain today.

Fifty years ago it was thought that adoption was a one-off event, a new start for all concerned and children, most of them small babies, could be brought up without knowing that they were adopted. Presumably grandparents and other relatives kept the secret and did their best to make the unrelated grandchild their own. We have now learned from adopted people, birth parents and adopters that adoption is never a one-off event but remains a significant life factor that has to be acknowledged and respected.

An adopted child will always be the child of two sets of parents. Most children adopted since the mid 1970s have been adopted from the public care system and have suffered losses and traumas. They come to adoption with both good and bad memories that cannot be jettisoned at will. Some of their parents will have neglected or abused them, but children can be attached to neglectful and abusive parents. Adults, even those who were adopted as infants, tell us that they grew up with a gap in their lives that could not be filled until they found out more details about their origins. Cutting off the past from the present and the future confuses a child's sense of identity; adopted children, like all children, need to understand where they came from and how they got to where they are. Openness, not secrecy, is at the heart of modern adoption. Adoptive grandparents can, helpfully, share some of the responsibility for maintaining continuity for their adopted grandchildren and for keeping them connected to their history.

Becoming related by adoption

While grandparents are increasingly finding a voice as workers, consumers, voters, pensioners, caregivers, and significant relatives of children in care, there is little recognition of the less conventional role grandparents may or may not play when their own children adopt. Becoming a grandparent, an aunt, an uncle or a cousin is an automatic consequence when an infant is born. Most of us can draw on experience and role models in the family to make a reasonably good job of it. But it is not the same as becoming related by adoption.

There are preparation and training courses for prospective adoptive parents. Every applicant has to participate in a "home study", which explores family networks and support systems. National Adoption Standards make continuing adoption support for the child, the adopters and the birth parents obligatory for every agency. But as far as grandparents and other relatives are concerned, although best social work practice will at least include an interview with adoptive grandparents-to-be, this is not a requirement and it is far from usual.

What then are grandparents to make of their children's plan to adopt? Are they expected to be as involved as they might be in the birth of a grandchild? Should they become as attached? As the awaited child is unlikely to be an infant, or there may be two or more children coming together, how will that affect existing family relationships? What happens if a child doesn't want to stay? Or if the prospective adopters find that they cannot cope and the placement disrupts? We have all heard funny stories about the small child who tells her mummy to send the new baby back to the shop when the novelty has worn off, but adopters may indeed decide to terminate the placement of a child. Can the grandparents and other relatives then remain in the picture? How do adoptive grandparents stand in relation to the birth grandparents and how many grandparents can one child have? What if the child is of a different culture, religion or ethnicity from the adopting family? What if "ready-made" children come with second marriages and are adopted by their step-parent – do the step-family's parents became step-grandparents? Or if adopting sons or daughters are gay or lesbian, do grandparents still count? And what if grandparents have their own life with no time to give?

This brief handbook aims to give grandparents-to-be and other relatives information about adoption today; it offers some facts about the children who need to be adopted and discusses how the wider family can support and be involved in building a family through adoption. Quotes are widely used to illustrate a point. Names and situations have been changed to preserve anonymity.

The stories of adopted children and their relatives are at the heart of the book. One chapter has been jointly written by a parent of a family group of 15 children, who has also become a grandmother, and her own parents who are now the grandparents and great-grandparents of the children and the children's children.

Grandparents and other relatives come in many versions. Some are warm and friendly and others are more distant and formal. Some enjoy children and others find it harder to relate to them. Some are in and out of each other's homes and some are only seen once a year or live too far away to be seen at all. Very few grandmothers nowadays sit knitting in rose-covered cottages while grandfathers tell tales of bygone days in front of the fire. Grandparents, like their daughters and sons, work, travel, separate, divorce and re-marry. Adopted children have to find their way around a strange new family circle inhabited by unknown members and find a place in it for themselves. Grandparents and other relatives have an important role to play in making room for an adopted child in this circle.

01

What exactly is adoption?

I want to be adopted so as I shall have a dad to give me away when I'm married.
Ten-year-old girl

Adoption is at least as old as the Bible. Moses was adopted by Pharaoh's daughter. The importance of continuity also seems to be an ancient issue, for Miriam, Moses' sister, smuggled their birth mother into the court to become his wet nurse. Although this was probably not an open adoption, because no one except Miriam and the infant Moses knew that the wet nurse was the mother, contact was maintained. This adoption also had other modern aspects: it was transracial, intercountry and the child was of a different religion.

Informal adoption has been a way of looking after children who cannot live with their birth family throughout known history. Stories about adopted children include Oliver Twist, the boy who was orphaned, who asked for more, and after great adversity was finally "adopted" by a single man who turned out to be his grandfather! And Daniel Deronda was secretly "adopted" by another single, older man. He was lovingly brought up in an alien country and culture and spent much of his adult life searching for his roots and his identity.

Legal adoption in the UK was introduced in the second quarter of the 20th century and until the 1970s, it was largely regarded as a service for infertile couples. There were plenty of babies available until better birth control, acceptance of single parenthood and illegitimacy reduced the numbers drastically. The Adoption Acts of the late 1970s (in England & Wales and Scotland) made it clear that adoption was no longer to be a service for couples but a service for children who needed a new family. It became easier to dispense with the birth parents' agreement to adoption on grounds of consent being unreasonably withheld. From now on, the child's needs and rights were to be paramount. These needs and rights have since been further defined in legislation throughout the UK.

02

The adoption process

*My daughter told us they were going to adopt.
Next thing we heard was, they were going to
adopt three together. Then they said they weren't
going to be babies. We didn't like to ask too much
but we didn't know what to expect or what was
expected of us.*
Parents of adopters

George Bernard Shaw wrote in *Everyone's Political What's What:*

> *Parentage is a very important profession but no test for it is ever imposed in the interests of children.*

He might have added:

> *unless you are going to adopt.*

The adoption process can be very stressful for people who are entering what can seem like a strange new world where no one can have children without being scrutinised – as they can in the real world – and where they will have to prove their competence to become parents.

At first we thought, 'What have we let ourselves in for?' But as it went on, we realised how much we had to learn.
Prospective adopters

The road to adoption may feel like a lonely journey and it is not always easy to ask for support from those who are nearest and dearest. There may be pain and embarrassment about the decision to adopt and a fear of becoming "different". However, if members of the extended family know what is happening, what the process entails; if they can remain patient and encouraging without seeming intrusive, then adoption can, in time, become a very special family event.

I know my mum wanted me to tell her all about it but I couldn't. I felt too choked half the time. Also I didn't know if we'd get through and I didn't want to raise her hopes. But she was always there for me. She sort of encouraged me by just being around like normal and waiting till I was ready to talk.
Prospective adopter

The diagram below shows the adoption process from first enquiry to the Adoption Order for both family and child.

The adoption process

ADOPTERS   **CHILD**

Expressing an interest		Looked after children review
Information meeting		Permanence plan agreed
Home visit		If the plan is for adoption
Application		BAAF Child Permanence & Medical Reports
Police & heath check		
Training & preparation		Adoption panel recommendation
Assessment (home study)		
Adoption panel		Family finding

Matching meeting & report

Adoption panel recommendation

Agency decision

Child appreciation day

Preparation for specific child

Introduction planning

Introduction review

Placement

Reviews of placement

Adoption application

Adoption order

The process of adoption can be broken down into six parts:

Enquiry
- A single person or couple decide that they want to adopt a child or children.
- They approach their local authority or a voluntary adoption agency in their area for information.
- They will be given written information about adoption, the agency, the preparation and training offered and the statutory requirements regarding health, and police checks and personal references. This information should be available in the main languages spoken in the locality.
- They may be invited to an Open Meeting held regularly for all enquirers or they may be offered a one-off consultation with a social worker to learn about the kind of children needing new families.

This is a good opportunity for relatives to be involved. Although they may not always suggest it, nearly all agencies would welcome first-time enquirers to bring friends or relations to an initial meeting. And there is never any harm in asking!

If the prospective adopters decide to proceed, they will be asked to join a Preparation or Training Group in due course.

Training
Groups of several couples and single people usually meet weekly for about six sessions. Or the agency may offer intensive whole days at weekends over a shorter period. Only a handful of agencies offer any training to grandparents and other relatives.

The training for prospective adopters will include:

- learning about how children become attached to their carers and how attachments can become disordered;

- issues of loss, separation and trauma;
- the significance of continuity, connection and contact for children who cannot live with their birth parents;
- why children need to be adopted and why families adopt;
- the experiences of families that have adopted;
- the meaning of family histories, systems and stories;
- health and education;
- the importance of a supportive network;
- anti-discriminatory practice in the family and the community.

It is helpful if family members know what is being covered in the training. An expression of interest in the written course material may lead to easier communication about the adoption plan.

After the training period, people will be asked to complete a formal application form if they wish to proceed. Because children must be protected, all prospective adopters have to agree to health, police and social services checks. References will then be followed up. **Adopters are asked to give the names of two personal referees, who know them well and are not related, but relatives can be named as additional referees; this offers an easy way of including them in the process.** However, applicants will be given every possible opportunity to withdraw at this point. Adoption is not for everyone.

Home study
This is the very personal and searching part of the process. It is not a study or assessment of the accommodation as is sometimes thought. If families feel comfortable in their homes, and as long as the physical surroundings don't pose a risk for a child, it is likely a child would also be comfortable. Standards of housekeeping should not be on trial and no one should feel the need to tidy up before the social worker arrives.

A social worker will visit the home several times to gather evidence of the applicants' competence and capacity to become parents by adoption. During this time, the prospective adopters may feel that their whole lives are under public scrutiny and that their privacy and dignity are under attack. In these circumstances it is not surprising if they withdraw from further discussion with members of their own family.

I was expected to talk about things I never think about. I suppose to begin with I was resentful really. Looking back it made me understand better about me as a child and what it would be like for a child having me as a Dad. But my family thought it was just social workers being nosy and so I never really talked to them about it. They never really caught on about adoption.
Prospective adopter

The home study will include an assessment of:

- family histories, life-styles and aspirations in relation to adoption;
- parenting experience and experience of being parented;
- reasons for childlessness and attitudes to infertility or wanting more children by adoption;
- relationship with partner if applicable and previous long-term relationships;
- support from the extended family, friends and community;
- ethnicity, culture and religious practice;
- attitude to openness towards birth family;
- ability to ask for help and work with agencies;
- employment, education and finance.

Relatives should be interviewed during this phase if they have been named as referees or if they will be expected to make a significant contribution to the placement.

*I told them from the start that my sister would look
after him from school till I come home. She lives
near and she's got two of her own and she doesn't
work and she offered. I can't afford to lose my job.
My social worker saw as much of my sister and her
husband as of me. I began to wonder 'who's going
to adopt?' But it's worked out all right and Jake's
got two new families for the price of one.*
Single parent adopter

At the end of the home study, the social worker and applicants will
write a report together for the agency's Adoption Panel. This panel,
made up of professionals and lay people all experienced in adoption,
will recommend whether the applicants should be approved as
prospective parents. Most panels will invite the applicants to come
and meet the members of the panel with their social worker when
their application is discussed. If the applicants are not approved, the
agency must give them information about how to appeal against
the decision. It can be hard for parents-in-waiting to have to ask for
"public approval" to start a family.

*We know social services have to look after the
children in the first place, but going to Panel made
us feel even more different from the rest of the
family. These strangers have to read everything
there is to know about you before they can
approve you. And even with our social worker
saying it would be all right, we were in a state for
the three weeks leading up to it and on the day
we were so nervous we were both sick. You can't
explain to people who've had their own children,
how it feels for your whole future to depend on an
official decision.*
Adoptive parent

Matching and preparation for a specific child or children

During the whole process so far, prospective adopters will have been thinking about the child or children they might adopt. They may already have identified a child from one of several photo-listing publications that feature profiles and photographs of children who need new families. These children will have gone through their own part of the adoption process (see diagram) and will be ready to be "matched" with a family.

There is no knowing for sure which child will be right for which family and surprising matches have been made and have worked out well. By this time, when prospective adopters have been approved, they will probably feel more confident about discussing possible children with family members. But beware about influencing their choice! It is rather like choosing a partner for life and chemistry must be allowed to play its part. On the whole, it is more helpful to encourage adopters to ask the right questions about a child that appeals to them, than to try to get them to make the right choice. If they are given all the information available about a child, they will be able to make an informed decision about whether they and the child should be "matched".

The most important element of the matching process is the preparation for having a specific child. How will this child fit into this family? Lack of information at this stage can cause the adoption to break down later. Adopters need every bit of available information to help them to decide whether they are the right family for a particular child. A good agency will organise a Child Appreciation Day to ensure that adopters have the opportunity to meet everyone who knows the child: present and previous carers, social workers, teachers, medical practitioners, health visitors, therapists and, of course, the birth family. They should be told all the known facts including the painful ones. They should have access to the child's files in social services and they should be given a record of all the child's moves, separations and losses. This can be an overwhelming time for adopters and interest from their parents and other relatives is usually appreciated, although there will be a fitting reluctance to share intimate details about a child and the birth parents when the child is not yet theirs. If information about a child is not forthcoming, a little prodding and support from relatives to give the prospective adopters the confidence to ask for what should be theirs by right, would not come amiss. Grandparents could offer to meet the child's birth grandparents at this point; in some cases where this has happened, a relatively stress-free route of communication has been established between the two families.

It may become necessary for the prospective adopters to withdraw if they discover that they would, after all, not be the right parents for this child. If they do, they will need all the support they can get because they may feel they are failing a child who needs them. But better by far to enable people to find out what they can and what they can't do now, than to encourage them to persevere with a placement that could easily disrupt.

My brother and sister-in-law went ahead with the two boys; they didn't ask us and we didn't say anything but we knew it wasn't right. That older boy's problems were way beyond what they would be able to cope with. In the end, they found out for themselves so we could just prop them up without interfering.
Brother of prospective adopters

Introduction and placement

Introductions are as long or as short as a piece of string. Everything will depend on the child's need and capacity to become familiar and comfortable with new people and new places. It has to be remembered that every move for the child, however positive, also means a separation from other familiar people and places.

Very often adopters regard introductions as private and personal and there may be a virtual "keep out" notice as far as the extended family is concerned.

I was ready to welcome this little girl into the family, just as I've welcomed all my other grandchildren but my son didn't give me a chance. She'd moved in before I met her and I don't think we ever got off on the right foot after that. She saw me as someone intruding instead of someone belonging.
Grandmother of a six-year-old adopted girl

I dreaded my mum coming round. She goes over the top and I was afraid she'd cluck all over them or ask them things or expect them to come and sit on her lap. In the end I talked to her about it and she was great. The children took to her straight away; they moved in for her as much as for us! And now she's the gran they never had.
Adoptive parent of sibling group

When children move in to a new home with new parents there is often a honeymoon period before life resumes as normal. And normal can range from the usual ups and downs of living with children to more downs and less ups than we are used to in ordinary family life.

This is the time when grandparents and other relatives can rally round to offer practical help while avoiding criticism of the children or of the parent's handling of the children. Babysitting, outings, washing and ironing, gardening, cooking a meal and giving lifts will be seen as more supportive than giving advice. And it is never helpful to tell adopters who are struggling with unusual situations that they are not unusual or that the children will settle down soon. On the other hand, a good listener to tales of many woes, but also of small triumphs, is mostly very welcome.

Dad isn't fussed about what the children do or don't do. He gets on with all the odd jobs around the house and he lets them help. If they mess up he'll tell them, not get on at them. Then he'll sit down and make a cup of tea and I tell him all the latest. He won't say much, but he listens and he nods and looks pleased when he hears about a little bit of progress one of them has made.
Single adoptive parent of two brothers

Adoption and post-adoption

The final step of the adoption process is the making of an Adoption Order in Court. Some adoptions go ahead pretty quickly, others are delayed for a variety of reasons: the child is not ready, the parents are not confident enough to proceed, the birth parents are contesting the application, the social workers have not completed the report, a document is missing or the Court is dealing with a backlog.

The child has to have been in placement for a specific time before an application for an Order can be made in the Court. An application for adoption can be made up to the day a child reaches the age of 18.

Sometimes an Adoption Order can reassure a child and calm a turbulent passage; or it can make a seemingly settled child feel secure enough to open the floodgates and let rip; or it can simply be a happy event in a family story. In any case, it is a cause for a family celebration that can be added to the rest of the annual rituals.

The adoption process ends with the Order but adoption will be a lifetime factor for the child and all the family members. This has long been recognised by adoption practitioners and has now been acknowledged by the policy makers. All adoption agencies have a duty to assess the adoption support needs of families, including financial support, and to make a plan accordingly. The term "adoption support" covers all the services required before and after an Order is made. The help that grandparents and other relatives can offer will be taken into account when adoption support plans are agreed.

We couldn't have done without all the help the agency gave us right up to the time she was 18. And then they kept in touch and helped out when we had problems with benefits and wheelchairs and things because they knew her and the adult disability team in our area didn't understand about adoption. But the best were my mum and dad. They were always there for us. They never complained about having a severely disabled grandchild. They love her, like we do, and you can't buy that.
Adopter of young person with multiple impairments

Some legal points

- Grandparents and other relatives have no legal rights regarding adopted or birth children of the family.
- Grandparents and other relatives can be named as guardians for an adopted child (or birth child) by the adoptive parents in their wills.
- Adopted children have the same inheritance rights as children born to the family.
- Adopted children have exactly the same legal status as children born to the family.
- If an adoption disrupts after an order is made, the child remains the legal child of the adoptive parents, unless another family adopts the child.
- If an adopted child comes into public care, the adopters retain parental responsibility. According to UK legislation and/or guidance, relatives and significant others have to be considered as carers before a child is placed outside the family network.
- It is usual for adopted children to take the adopters' family name, but it is not a requirement. Older children sometimes prefer to keep their names or to add the adopters' name to their own.
- An adopted child does not retain a legal connection to their birth parents.

- An adopted person living in England, Wales or Northern Ireland has the right to identifying information about their birth family when they are 18. In Scotland, the age is 16.
- Legislation in England, Wales and Scotland allows two single people, of the same or different sex, to adopt together if they are in an established relationship. This is currently not the case in Northern Ireland.
- Under adoption legislation in England and Wales, birth parents have the right to approach specified agencies for information about their adopted child when that child reaches the age of 18. In Scotland and Northern Ireland there is no such legal right, but birth parents can request and receive a similar service.

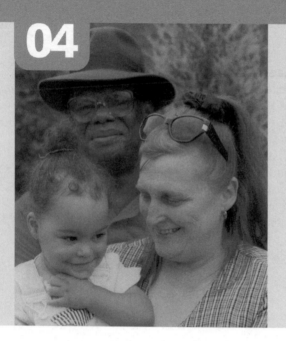

Who are the children?

I knew there weren't enough babies to go round, but I never knew there were so many children waiting to be adopted.
Adoptive grandparent of three sisters

Children, like families, come in all shapes and sizes and every child is unique. That is why it is not possible to say what kind of child parents will adopt; there is no "kind of child". An eight-year-old could have the emotional age of a toddler and the intellectual ability of a child of ten.

Tanya, aged seven, followed her new mum everywhere including the toilet and would not be left alone for a moment. Bedtime was agony for her because she knew that as soon as she fell asleep, she would be abandoned. Whenever she woke up in the night, she crept into her new parents' bed. Although she hated to leave her mother to go to school, she was easily top of the class and had a reading age of 12.

The few healthy babies who need to be adopted are usually placed with young childless couples but there are not enough babies to go around. Some people, who only want very young children, adopt them from overseas, but this is an expensive and uncertain business. It is also the case that many more of the poorer nations are striving to keep their children in their own country while, at the same time, the law regarding adoption of children from overseas has become more stringent in the UK.

Most of the children adopted today have been taken away from their birth parents. They come from all ethnic backgrounds and may have a mixed heritage. They may have been neglected or rejected; they may have parents who are too sick to care for them; they may have been emotionally, physically or sexually abused by members of their own family or their family may have been unable to protect them from abuse by others. Many of these children are part of a sibling group; some have mild to severe disabilities and some have been diagnosed with behavioural difficulties like ADHD (attention deficit hyperactivity disorder) or with an attachment disorder (a damaged capacity to make meaningful relationships due to earlier experiences). At some point, a court will have decided that these children would be at risk of significant harm if they returned to their homes. Nearly all of them will have been living with foster families and many of them will have moved several times while in foster care.

Children who have been born with a physical, sensory or intellectual impairment may need new families because their parents are not able to cope with disability or, in rare cases, they may even have caused the impairment. Bringing a disabled child into a family makes for a special kind of adoption. Parents have to want that child because of, and not in spite of, the impairment. Disabled children must never be regarded as second best but they do need a family that will fight for their rights, for their benefits, for their education and health care, for their social inclusion and for their transition to independence. Enough to keep the whole extended family busy!

Never lose sight of the child

It is possible to get carried away by trying to be honest about the children who need new families, but by focusing on their pain and problems, we may lose sight of the child. Like all children, these are also chatty, giggly, generous, gentle, funny, kind, quick, slow, robust, resilient, energetic and, above all, brave. They have possibly faced up to more hurt and disappointment than most of us have to deal with in a lifetime. It is important for everyone in the family to understand something about the history of children who are adopted from care but it is also important to respect the new parents' concern about protecting their new child. It isn't necessary for every relation to know every single detail from the very beginning in order to feel related.

We didn't exactly hide anything about Liam, we gave my parents the general idea, but we didn't go into the gory details. We thought it would best come out when he was ready to talk about it himself. And he did – once he got used to his new Nanna, he told her things even we didn't know. It was a good job she was prepared for it or it would have knocked her sideways.
Adopter of four-year-old boy

It has to be self-evident that children who have had a hard time are not going to be easy to bring up. They will need patience and a great deal of consistent care and attention before they can learn to trust their new family and the world around them. This new world will include not only parents, but grandparents, uncles, aunts, cousins and a medley of other relatives.

We would like a child joining a new family to be able to say with Miranda from Shakespeare's *The Tempest:*

O, wonder!
How many goodly creatures are there here!
How beauteous mankind is! O brave new world
That has such people in't! (Act 5 Scene 1)

Family systems and circles

I've got an old Nan and a new Gran but I don't know how to fit them together.
Adopted boy aged seven

Every family tells a story. Or several stories, or the same story from different angles. We grow up with our family stories; we also grow up learning slowly who all the characters are: who is who in the family circle. Members of this circle may never be seen by the child growing up, but if they appear in the family stories, they will nevertheless be known as "uncle Harry with the large ears" or "cousin Midge who happens to be very tall".

Holding collective memories

Grandparents and other older relatives are usually the main storytellers in the family. They hold the collective memories. In some cultures where there is a strong oral tradition, the elders of the tribe are revered because they alone pass on the history of the family, the community and the nation. Hence there is a deep respect for old age and the wisdom of experience. In Western societies there is no such built-in respect for elders – the elders have to earn it. They must be tactful, may not interfere, be available when needed, avoid giving advice but be ready to share what they have learned. If they tell their stories too often, someone will soon say: 'Oh Grandma, you've told us that a dozen times'. Nevertheless, most families value their stories; they return to them again and again and build on them as they go along.

Entering the family circle

How will a child enter the family circle and catch up with the stories? New parents may be too busy with the many aspects of the parenting-by-adoption task to fill the child in with what other children learn from the cradle. They might welcome an offer of help from grandparents or other relatives – as long as they are kept in the picture.

One afternoon a week could be spent with older relations for the express purpose of introducing the child to the family circle and family stories in quite a direct way. Old family photographs are good triggers for storytelling; grandfathers should never be overlooked as storytellers; mementoes can be shared with the child and treasures can be shown on these special occasions: a school report, a certificate for an achievement, a card made for an anniversary long ago, a milk tooth or a lock of baby hair preserved, a remembrance of a loved pet, a medal belonging to an uncle killed in a war. Not all memories have to be happy ones. The child is joining a real family, not a fairy tale.

Listening to new family stories and being absorbed into a new family circle should give children the opportunity to share some of their own stories and to make connections between the two. If children can acknowledge where they have come from, and learn to value the good bits of their past while letting go of the bad bits, then they will be able to concentrate better on their new family. There's a lot of catching up to do when children are adopted – the child has to catch up with the family and the family has to catch up with the years the child was elsewhere. Grandparents and other relatives have an essential inter-generational role to play.

I fetched her from school on Thursdays and she came to my place. We made a ritual out of it. First there was milk and a different cake I made for her every week. She liked to know about baking so we wrote the recipes out together and pasted them into a folder that she kept in my kitchen with my cookery books. Then it was the family albums. She always remembered where we'd left off the last time but more often than not she wanted to go back a bit or start again from the beginning. Sometimes she asked that many questions, it set me off on memory lane, so we only had time to look at a couple of pages before it was time to take her home.
Grandparent of an adopted ten-year-old girl

Every family is different

There is yet more to accomplish for the child entering the new family circle. Every family has its own lifestyle, its own system, as well as its own stories. No one family has quite the same way as any other of dealing with health, education, work, money, travel, discipline, noise, cleanliness, order, food, leisure, illness, hospitality and everything else that makes them who they are. The value put on healthy eating, for instance, the rules about sitting up at the table or the rituals for making mealtimes shared occasions for exchanging the news of the day, will vary tremendously between families.

Tracy had mostly chips in paper bags with her birth mum. Her foster carer was very strict about eating at regular times sitting up at the table with the other children. Now she can't figure out how to handle our more casual style of eating together, on our laps, at different times to suit the working members of the family. She goes frantic if a meal is late; she always wants to know what the rules are even when there aren't any.
Prospective adopter of a six-year-old girl

And this is only one aspect of dozens that may be confusing Tracy about her new family's system. Even the meaning of well-known words may become obscure. What does this family mean by "keeping in touch" for example? Does it mean talking on the phone daily, keeping an "open house" for family members, friends and neighbours, visiting by invitation, sending birthday cards, writing letters and emails or meeting only at family celebrations and times of crisis? When they meet, do they hug, kiss, shake hands or avoid physical contact?

And, most relevant for grandparents and other older relatives, how do the generations interact? How do the branches of the family tree hold together? Children who come from dysfunctional families will have to learn how this one functions properly, that some branches of the tree are more frail than others but that they will survive because the tree is strong. Grandparents and other relatives are important players in this new system and can help to guide the new child through what may seem to be an incomprehensible maze of values, standards and behaviours.

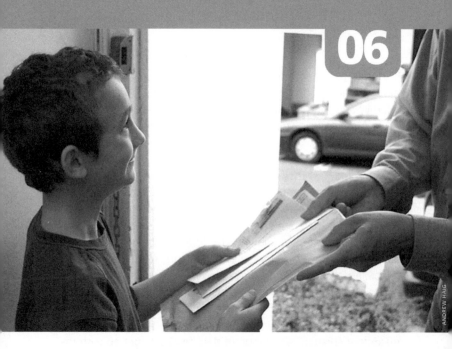

06

Continuity, connection and contact

A ten-year-old boy became devoted to the postman because it was he who brought letters from his brothers and sisters.

It used to be thought that adoption was a neat solution for the birth mother who couldn't look after her child, for the child who needed a family and for the childless adopters. All three parties to adoption could make a clean start and forget all about the birth, the rejection and the infertility. Over the years, we have learned, from the people themselves, that those who have been adopted need to know who they are and why they are where they are, that adopters have to negotiate and celebrate a different way of building a family and that birth mothers never forget. There may be momentous changes, like adoption, but there are no fresh starts in life: we can only begin life once and finish it once and we have to make the most of the bit in between; we have to carry our baggage and create a whole life by remaining connected to both ends. We can't live a healthy life in pieces. "She's gone to pieces" is an accurate description of someone who can't hold their life together. Anything we try to cut out of our story has a habit of hitting back at us. But this doesn't mean that children can't let go of their fears and get on with their new life.

We thought it best to let bygones be bygones and we agreed we'd never talk about his dad to our adopted son unless he brought it up himself. Danny was scared of him, we knew that, but he was going to be in prison for years. It was all in the past and Danny knew he was safe with us.

It wasn't until Danny had been with us for a year that he started having these terrible nightmares. He was dreaming about this big animal climbing up the drainpipe and getting him – he'd wake up screaming. From things he said, we thought he was having nightmares about his dad coming to get him. So we started to talk about what had happened to him. How we wouldn't let anyone hurt him but how we couldn't take away the hurt his dad had done. We told him that he didn't have to worry about it happening again and he didn't have to pretend it never happened.

After a bit he calmed down and the nightmares stopped gradually. Then one day he said, 'I think about my dad a lot but I'm not scared any more. When I'm bigger I'd like to go and see if he's OK.'
Adopters of an eight-year-old boy

We sometimes talk about going back to our roots; plants have roots, people have legs and can move. Children can move to new families without lasting damage but the transition has to be managed without breaking the thread of continuity with the past and the connection to their birth family.

The need for connection

Children's need for connection and continuity may, or may not, lead to contact with the birth family after they are placed for adoption. And contact can range from face-to-face visits arranged by the two families themselves to an annual exchange of news through a third party – usually the adoption agency that arranged the placement. Contact may have to be supervised by social workers to protect the child and the adopters should be aware of what is said on the telephone, in text messages, emails and social networks. This becomes more difficult when children are teenagers and is a good example of how the adoption factor can make a difference to family life. Use of the internet could lead to unplanned contact between adopted children and their birth families.

If contact is deemed to be unsafe or undesirable for children, there are ways of keeping absent people in mind that do not pose a danger.

Ruby, aged 12, and her sister Jade, aged ten, had frightening memories of their mother who was a long-term patient in a psychiatric hospital. They visited her once with their adoptive parents and were distressed because she didn't recognise them. They were also relieved to see that she was being looked after at last. Ruby told her mother's social worker, 'We don't have to see her because our new mum's put our old mum in the family circle, so we won't lose her'.

Contact plans

A plan for contact with the birth family has to be considered for every child placed for adoption. The purpose of contact has to be clear and the plan has to be in the child's interests. Questions of where, when, how often and with whom, should be negotiated with the adopters. And it is always important to hear the views of the children – only they can tell us about their most meaningful connections. Very often they will include current and past carers who may have played as significant a part in their lives as their birth family.

It is a mistake to think that children need to "settle" in the adoptive home before they have any contact with the people from their past life. On the contrary, they will settle more easily and be more confident if the links are preserved from the beginning. Imagine getting married and being told that in order to make the marriage work, you may not hear or see any of your other loved ones for three months at least! You could blame and resent your new partner for imposing such conditions!

At best, contact with birth relatives and other significant people is like seeing members of your extended family – you like some more than others – sometimes family occasions work and sometimes they don't – but that's families for you. At worst, there can be conflict and then outside help should be available to mediate and negotiate more acceptable contact arrangements. Sometimes children are upset before and after meetings and this has been used as a reason for terminating contact. It may be that there are specific reasons for the upset, which should be explored, or it may be that children need more preparation and more support, but very rarely is it an indication for contact to stop. We must allow children to feel sad and to be upset; they can't be happy all the time.

Where do grandparents and other relatives come in to these contact arrangements?

Perhaps they are well placed to take some of the heat out of the event. Contact can be a stressful experience for both sets of parents as well as for the child and, as in other family situations, the presence of less intensely involved members of the family can be a calming and supportive influence.

When it was time for one of those contact meetings, we always made a family occasion of it. We'd plan a picnic or some kind of outing and it would be the children and my daughter and son-in-law and me; Beryl (birth mother) would bring her mother along and that made it easier for the children; it opened it out more somehow and they could see that we all got on together. Their granny was a nice woman but very shy. The children really liked seeing her but I don't think she'd have come if I hadn't been there. The younger one said to us at one contact meeting, 'How many grannies am I allowed to have?'
Grandparent of three

07

Ethnicity, religion and culture

They're not really the same as me but they're not really different.
Eight-year-old African-Caribbean child adopted by black mixed heritage parents

If you had to describe yourself, long distance, to an alien on another planet, what would you say? What is important about the way you look, move, behave, dress, eat and sleep? Do your own family, the community you belong to, the language you speak and the country you live in have some bearing on who you are? Are your beliefs and values, the way you feel and relate to others, also part of you? How will you convey what you mean? If you tell the alien that you are white or black, will he understand that white means anything from pink to beige and black means anything from olive to dark brown?

Although new families are not aliens from another planet, children joining a new family easily feel bemused or puzzled by an unfamiliar culture, religious practice or if the family is of a different ethnicity to their own, and find it hard to explain themselves or to hold on to their own picture of themselves. It is therefore the aim of adoption agencies to match the child as closely with a family as is possible. We have learned how vital it is for children's sense of identity and self-esteem to grow up in families that can embrace and share their cultural, religious and ethnic heritage. But ethnicity, religion and culture do not define the whole person, as our alien would testify, and sometimes the need for a family must over-ride other considerations.

Even if a child comes from exactly the same minority ethnic background as the adopters, the two mothers might come from different communities or tribes or sects or castes from within the same country. The fathers might vary from pale to dark of the same skin colour. Then there is religion: a Protestant Christian from Cheltenham is not the same as a Protestant Christian from Northern Ireland. There are many accepted versions of each of the major religions and there are less well-known alternative faiths. Class and culture can be even more confusing: Does it matter how we speak? What do we read or watch on television? Which sport do we play or follow? Do we live for the day or plan for tomorrow?

Dana, aged 11, said about her new family: 'They're not too bad but they speak posh, they don't watch Big Brother, they don't know nothing about football and we're always having to go to the library. Then they make me save half my pocket money. I don't know why. But I like them 'cause they're nice. And there's all the aunts and uncles and grandma and that – they're all like that – but they're nice too.'
Black child adopted by black family

What can grandparents do?

So how can grandparents and other relatives help adopted children to strengthen their own identities? To appreciate similarities and also acknowledge that they are different from new family members? Never suggest that differences don't matter or will not be noticed – that could make a child feel insignificant or even invisible. It is better to talk about the difference and to find a way to celebrate it.

Grandpa Ron and me used to make a point of telling Josie how much we admired her hair. I took a course on how to braid Afro hair and then we used to spend hours trying out different styles. It really takes hours and I think my daughter-in-law was pleased I could do it because she works and doesn't have the time – although she's African and we're not. Josie was ten when she came to us and she's 14 now but she still comes to me to have her hair done. It gives us a closeness we wouldn't have had otherwise. Grandpa Ron always comes to look when we've finished and she loves it when he

approves. He takes photos to keep a record of all
the different styles.
Adoptive grandparent

Other relatives may like to become experts on the various festivals
and rituals to which the child has been accustomed and help to
provide the right food and venue at the right time to celebrate as a
family.

At one time we only had family get togethers at
Christmas and birthdays but now we have
adoption days and Chinese New Year as well. I
make the jiaozi (New Year dumplings) and get all
the bits and pieces like chocolate money stuffed in
red envelopes and I decorate the house with
special Chinese banners. To begin with it was more
for my adopted nieces, but now we're all getting
more interested in their background and we're all
kind of discovering about it together.
Adoptive aunt

There are as many ways of communicating with children about who
they are, as there are ways of describing ourselves to aliens. Some
ways will work better than others, but the important thing is to take
every opportunity to keep on trying.

08

Common problems, questions and some answers

Can I be a real grandparent to unrelated children – will I be able to love them?

It is natural and usual for grandparents to love their grandchildren. They won't necessarily love them all the same and some may live far away but, on the whole, they often enjoy a special relationship with their grandchildren because they don't have the responsibility of bringing them up. Unless they offer regular childcare to enable their children to work, they can spoil them and "hand them back" when they've had enough! Grandchildren bring renewal to the whole family; their birth signals hope for the future and for the survival of the tribe. Of course, a great part of the pleasure they give to the family has to do with watching their development from babyhood: 'hasn't he grown?' or 'she's always been a smiler' and with their likeness to someone else: 'you are the image of your mother at the same age' or: 'just like your father – can't wait for anything'. But how will it be if the adopted child is older or disabled, troubled by past events and has another family? And how about being faced with two, three or even more sisters and brothers one by one or even all at the same time?

It was hard for my mother to accept the idea of adopting disabled children. But once she got over the initial shock, she grew very fond of them and used to call Robert and Claude 'my boys'. She was anxious for us the first time and the second, but by the time we took Corena she'd given up worrying. She'd always said that she didn't want her grandchildren to call her "nanna" – she wanted to be "gran" or "grandma" – but they all called her "nanna" and she liked it.
Adoptive parent in *Whatever Happened to Adam?*
BAAF, 1998

It is not always easy for grandparents to accept their adult children's infertility. Their feelings of disappointment and their sense of loss and discontinuation often remain unacknowledged because they are not the main players in the adoption scenario.

Betsy was adopted. For her eighth birthday, she and her mother had decided to make Betsy's room into a big girl's room. They chose wallpaper and paint and fabric for curtains and did the whole room by themselves. They had great fun and were both excited and pleased with the result. The grandparents were there for Betsy's birthday dinner. After the cake, Betsy and her mother each took one of Nana's hands and told her to close her eyes and they would lead her to a surprise. They walked her down the hallway to the bedroom door and told her to open her eyes. She did. She looked around the room and finally said, 'What a beautiful room for someone else's child'.
(From *The Family of Adoption* by Joyce Maguire Pavo, Boston: Beacon Press, 1998)

I don't suppose this grandmother meant to be so terribly unkind. She was probably even unaware of her sadness that Betsy was not her generic grandchild. She may have been a perfectly caring and loving grandmother for most of the time. But being aware about adoption issues and feelings that may recur is essential to the well-being of the adoptive family.

My daughter has adopted five children so I'm their adopted grandmother. I think you can learn to be an adoptive grandparent but it's not the same as when I had my two children and their nannas were there from the beginning – right there in the hospital and it just grew from that. If your adult children adopt a baby it could be the same but not if they come older. You have to fit in more with what they need. I've been upset – very, very upset – when there have been real problems but you can't interfere. You've got to be there for them but you mustn't expect too much.
Nanna by adoption in *Be My Parent*, April 1999

Some adopted children may avoid close relationships with new parents to begin with and find it easier to relate to a comfortable old grandparent, a more distant aunt or an accepting new cousin, preferably one at a time. Other children will cope best in the hurly burly of a large, open family where everybody comes and goes and they can get by without being noticed too much. If grandparents and other relatives can "fit in more with what they need", there is a good chance that love will grow in time. And if not love, then respect and concern for a young person who has lost one family and is brave enough to risk having another. It may never feel the same as having related grandchildren, nieces, nephews or cousins, but the difference can be enriching and lead to a wider appreciation of the family circle.

Will an older child learn to love their new family?

Children can love many adults, especially if the adults respect each other and tell the same story. We have learnt from divorce that it is more difficult for children to maintain positive emotional ties with adults who are hostile to each other.

It used to be thought that children could transfer their attachments from one group of people to another and that we had to help them to detach from their birth families or previous carers before they could attach to adopters. But this doesn't make sense. In real life we don't have to jettison an old friend before we make a new one. Nor do we lose our own family when we become a member of our partner's family. As the saying goes: 'You're not losing a daughter but gaining a son'. In fact, from infancy on we learn to extend our attachments, not to exchange one for another. Healthy infants extend their attachments from their main carer to the rest of the family and, step-by-step, to significant people in the outside world. It is a process of building more relationships, not of weeding them out. Children who have been in the care system have already sustained losses and we must help them to retain as many of their previous relationships as is compatible with their safety and wellbeing.

It is then not a matter of changing from the old to the new, but of changing the balance between the old and the new. Picture a seesaw. At the beginning of the road to adoption, the weight is with the birth family and/or previous carers while the adopters are up in the air. The child starts off where the weight is and gradually has to work her or his way towards the adopters so that the weight will shift to them and their end of the seesaw will touch the ground. It is a difficult journey and often there are obstacles to negotiate. There is usually a spurt to begin with (known as the "honeymoon"), until the child reaches the middle of the seesaw where she or he is likely to get stuck for a bit with both families hovering at the same level on either side. At this point it may look as though the child is battling to keep control of the seesaw and perhaps would like to say: 'Hold on to me – don't let me go'. If the child is safely held, the slow move towards investing wholeheartedly in the new family can follow.

What are the obstacles some adopted children face?

Disordered attachments

Attachments become disordered if children are hurt, neglected, rejected or abandoned by the very people who should be caring for them. Instead of healthy attachments that can be extended, these children tend to form insecure attachments that lead to difficulties in making new relationships. They may make excessive demands on the one hand or avoid any form of closeness on the other. They have no safe pattern to follow.

It was like Jonathan wasn't really with us. He was living in the house and he wasn't much trouble but he kept us at a distance. It was bad enough for us, we'd been warned to expect it, but my mother kept trying to draw him out and getting hurt by what he said to her. He told her to shut up because she wasn't his real grandma. We had to explain to her why he was like that. I think it took nearly a year before he could respond and then it was only for some of the time with some people. Adopter of ten-year-old boy, Jonathan

I was hurt when Jonathan said I wasn't his real grandma, but when my son explained about him I could see that I wasn't as hurt as he had been. Jonathan's grandmother

What a pity the grandmother wasn't included in the preparation so that she could support the parents through a particularly stressful period.

Lack of trust

Children who have been repeatedly let down by adults are not trusting. They cannot take it for granted that they will not be let down again and it may be easier for them not to risk it. Building their trust in the new family is a major task in which all family members can participate. Small things matter: making promises and keeping them, always turning up at the school gates on time, keeping confidences, hearing what the child says, being loyal to the child and to their new parents, remembering birthdays and anniversaries, being consistent about praise and discipline and being available.

I remember I was really rude to my grandma when I was first adopted. She kept on and on at me to talk to her and she really got on my nerves. But she went on coming to see me and brought me things even when I was rude, and now we're really good friends because I know I can trust her.
Jonathan, aged 12

Unfinished business

If children are moved into an adoptive placement without enough preparation, they will arrive confused and unable to make the transition without becoming disturbed and creating disturbance. They will be trying to deal with "unfinished business". If they have had to say "goodbye" to their birth family they may blame the adopters for asking the impossible. If they have had to leave a loved foster family too abruptly, the loss could outweigh gaining a new family. If they have been separated from brothers and sisters, they may be preoccupied with becoming reunited. If they do not know or cannot make sense of their own story, they will not make sense of their new situation. There is no substitute for adequate preparation for children – and the same is true of adopters – but sometimes the new family has to do this work in retrospect, as well as they can. Whatever the age and understanding of a child, ways can be found to communicate and to explore together, the road the child has travelled to be adopted.

Auntie Annie was always making things for all the children in the family. When Alison, aged five, was adopted, she seemed not to understand what was happening to her. She repeatedly asked for her previous carers. Auntie Annie made paper dolls to represent all the people Alison had lived with. She got Alison to describe them and to decide what clothes they should wear. Then she made a special box for the dolls where they could be safe. Alison seemed to be totally pre-occupied with these dolls and wouldn't play with any of the other toys the adopters had prepared for her. She talked to the dolls and slept with them under her pillow. After a few days, Auntie Annie added dolls for Alison's new family and made a second special box for them. To begin with, Alison wouldn't play with the new dolls. Then she slowly included them one at a time in her games until they were all mixed up together and living in the same box. She used the other box for their spare clothes that Auntie Annie kept on supplying to order. Only then, did Alison start playing with other toys.

Every child placed for adoption should have a life story book – a record, with photographs, drawings and maps of each person and place and event that have featured in their life so far. Life story books can be shared and read over and over again with additional explanations and they can be updated to include the present and to draw the child's life into a continuous whole. That is the ideal! Unfortunately, not all life story books are complete or comprehensive; many avoid the painful bits of the story and some are no more than photograph albums. But it is never too late to augment a life story book or even to begin a new one. *My Life and Me* and *Me and My Family*, (by Jean Camis/Jean Maye, published by BAAF, 2001 and 2011) are useful tools to get going with some simple, interactive ideas.

Children may feel very reluctant about sharing their life story with members of their new family but, in due course, it will be reassuring and confirming for them to know that not only parents, but other relatives have also included their story in the family history.

"Into moves"

Some children have been moved so often that moving itself becomes the name of the game. You never have to make the best or the most of anything because there will be another move soon. Moves are exciting because you never know what you will find and the grass just might be greener next time. These children have no concept of permanence and usually move without a backward glance. People mistakenly think that they have settled quickly because the move has been painless, but in truth, children who are "into moves" see themselves as merely passing through.

On the day she moved to her adoption placement, seven-year-old Leila said to her social worker: 'Next time I'd like a family by the seaside'.

The intended permanence of adoption has to be demonstrated and emphasised continuously. All the family members can help: talking about events in the future, planning future holidays together, looking ahead to family celebrations, discussing choices in education, making long-term arrangements for health care and buying winter clothes in the summer or vice versa will all contribute to giving children a sense of staying where they are.

How will the child fit in with existing grandchildren, nephews and nieces?

Generally children will accept half-siblings, stepsiblings and adopted siblings if the parents and the rest of the family are comfortable with the situation. The same applies to grandchildren, nephews and nieces. There may be rivalry and jealousy but this also happens in the most regular and best-regulated families. It is no good pretending that love will be instant or that the new arrival will have an equal share of it from the word go. In any case, there are no equal shares of love. But the idea that love can grow for all concerned gives children the opportunity to participate in devising ways and means to make it grow.

We get on well with all our grandchildren. We see them most weeks and I suppose we do spoil them. When our daughter adopted the twins – they were just four years old, the same as our youngest grandson – we got all our grandchildren together and worked out how to make the twins feel they belonged. The children had some good ideas and it made them include the twins straight away. My oldest grand-daughter was nearly 15 and she kind of took charge. I think the twins learned about grandparents from the other children. They soon expected special treats along with the rest of them but you could see that it really made them happy.
Grandparent with nine grandchildren, two adopted

This grandmother has photographs of all her grandchildren displayed in her sitting room. The adopted twins have been given a prominent place.

What is meant by "behaviour problems"?

When children are said to have behaviour problems it usually means more than high spirits, toddler temper tantrums, adolescent rudeness, routine naughtiness or just being stroppy. Children who feel rejected or insecure, who have been neglected or abused, who lack a sense of continuity or self-worth, will communicate their pain through their behaviour. In other words: if children are disturbed, their behaviour will become disturbing; if they feel they have no control over their own lives, they will attempt to impose control on others by any means in their power.

Lying, stealing, bed-wetting, soiling, unprovoked anger and aggression or complete withdrawal are symptoms of distress and cries for help. Very often a child's emotional development is arrested by bad experiences. Any of the behaviours listed above might be acceptable for a three-year-old, but would be considered as problematic for an older child.

When my brother and his wife adopted Cindy, they were over the moon. Then she started all this business with screaming if she didn't get her own way. She clings to my sister-in-law, won't leave her alone for a minute. She can't play on her own and she upsets other children. It's embarrassing because she behaves like a baby though she's a big girl. Last birthday I took them all out to the seaside with my children and we had a really good day. For once Cindy didn't try to get the others into trouble – they all got on like an ordinary family. Then on the way home, she got cross for no reason and did her screaming all the way back and upset everybody. She spoiled the outing. And you can never get her to say 'sorry'.
Uncle of adopted girl of nine

Children who have been hurt find it very hard to show remorse when they hurt others. If they feel bad about themselves, they may have to spoil anything good that happens to them because they feel they don't deserve it and they can't trust that it will last. It took Cindy three years in a loving home before she felt secure enough to act her age and to give real affection.

Many families enjoy an initial "honeymoon" when children are first placed for adoption. It can take some while for a child to feel safe enough to reveal their troubled self. There is hardly ever a straight course between problems and resolution of problems. There may be times of relative calm interspersed with difficulties; there may be consistent progress with three steps forward and two steps back; there may be a trouble free run of years only to be followed by a particularly turbulent adolescence.

Grandparents and other relatives can show that they understand why a child behaves in a certain way while at the same time supporting the parents to hang on and to get through it. They can best support the children by accepting that they are stuck at a certain stage of emotional development and by having faith that they will not remain stuck there forever.

How will we cope with a disabled child?

If single parents or couples adopt a child with disabilities, they will have had the opportunity to think long and hard about the changes a disabled child will bring to the family. Hopefully the plan to adopt a child with disabilities will also have been discussed with grandparents and other relatives who may become involved. It is important to add a disabled child to the family not "in spite of" but "because of" the disability.

*I explained to my family that we wanted to adopt
Ricky because he was a baby with Down's
Syndrome. We've been ordinary parents to
ordinary children and we were ready to do
something for a special child who needed a family
more. My dad kept saying it was second best but it
wasn't. It was best for Ricky and it was best for us.
Now he's best for the whole family.*
Adoptive parent

Another adoptive mother explained that just as every child is
unique, so is every disability.

*What you have to do is to find the beauty spot –
that something or other that makes each child
special. For me it's Joe's silence that says more than
if he could speak.*

Relatives by adoption may also be able to find the beauty spot of
children with disabilities.

What about children from overseas?

Children adopted from overseas may be younger than most children
needing adoption in the UK. However, they are even more likely to
have suffered severe emotional if not physical deprivation in early
infancy. They may be from a different ethnic background than the
adoptive family; they may speak or be used to hearing a different
language; they may be familiar with a different religion, with
different customs, food and climate. If children are adopted from
overseas, they will grow up in their new family with three basic
questions: Why didn't my parents keep me? Why didn't my people

keep me? Why didn't my country keep me? This is a heavy load to carry into a new life. Grandparents and other relatives can help to support children from overseas by learning about their country and valuing their culture, so that they can grow up with pride in their origins and confidence in their status as adopted people and citizens of an adopted country.

What help is available?

Adoption law in England and Wales requires all adoption agencies to agree an adoption support plan when a child is placed with a new family. Adoption support can come in a variety of ways and from various directions. Specialist workers from social services, health and education can make valuable contributions. Both material and practical support should be on offer until the child is 18 – later if the young person is disabled.

Being prepared to accept help is as important as having the right help available. Sometimes adopters can feel that they have failed as parents if they ask for help. Or relatives can imply that there is something "wrong" if the adopted child is referred for therapy. Play therapy, drama therapy, art therapy and psychotherapy can guide a confused child towards putting their life together and help the parents and the extended family to support the child.

I was shocked when my son told me Ailsa was going to be seen at the clinic by a therapist. No one in the family has ever needed anything like that. She went twice a week for more than a year. My son and his wife used to go to see another person. I can see the improvement though I was against it.
Adoptive grandparent

Grandparents and other relatives can play a vital role in providing adoption support, not least by reassuring the parents that it is normal to seek outside help. After all, even grandparents can seldom draw on their own experience when adoption issues arise.

Will adopted stepchildren be my grandchildren/ nieces/nephews?

If the caretaking parent remarries, the new husband or wife can apply to adopt the children if the other birth parent agrees. Adopted stepchildren have the same legal status in the family as any other adopted children or, indeed, children born to the family.

In many cases there are more appropriate ways than adoption to secure the future for children from previous relationships. The Adoption and Children Act 2002 encourages stepfamilies to consider alternative arrangements to adoption in order to preserve the legal connection with the absent parent. Grandparents and other relatives then have to negotiate how best to include the children of previous marriages or partnerships in the extended family. Much will depend on the attitudes and expectations of the parents and on the existing extended families of the children.

How do relatives fit in if gay or lesbian couples adopt?

Children grow up successfully in all kinds of families. Lesbian and gay partners can adopt jointly in England, Wales and Scotland, and there is evidence that lesbian and gay couples can be excellent parents and that they and their children need the support of relatives as much as other parents do. It is, of course, important to know and to appreciate how the parents tell their story and how the child understands it. Children will feel comfortable in almost any truly caring situation as long as the adults are comfortable and co-

By the time Gail and I decided to adopt, my
parents had long accepted her into the family. They
greeted our announcement with the supportive
trepidation with which they tended to greet all my
"Big Plans". My parents had no grandchildren
when we started on the adoption trail, so they
were excited at the prospect but a little nervous
about what kind of rollercoaster ride I intended to
take them on. My father thought it good that we
were going to be out because he is absolutely
obsessed with being honest. At the same time, he
was worried about how homophobic society is,
and concerned that we might face a lot of hurt
and disappointment. It was hard for them to see
the struggle we had at times during the process.
From *Is it True you have Two Mums?* by Ruby Clay,
BAAF, 2010

operative. Criticism or disapproval of the parents' lifestyle, however
covert, will not do; it would be better to deal with any negative
attitudes before building a relationship with an adopted child.

I couldn't see how they would let my son adopt. I
was worried about the boy turning out gay and
social services blaming my son. I was sort of
ashamed about being his grandmother and I made
him call me by my first name. This went on for a
long time, it must have been five years, till the boy
himself said to me: 'I haven't got a mother but I'd
like for you to be my grandmother'. I realised then
that I'd been his grandmother in all but name and
that he and my son were more clever about it than
I was.
Grandparent of adopted teenager

What happens if an adoption doesn't work out?

Families and children have to know from the beginning of the adoption adventure that, in spite of the best of intentions and the best of preparation, there can be no guarantee that every adoption will work because no one can really know how it will be and how it will feel when this child moves in with this family. If an adoption breaks down, it is good practice to call it a "disruption". This means that it is not the end of the road for a child but an interruption in the child's journey to a permanent placement.

A disruption is hardly ever anyone's fault. It is usually a combination of unidentified, misinterpreted, and unpredictable circumstances. For instance: no one knew the extent of abuse the child had suffered, the adopters were less tolerant of deviant behaviour than expected and the promised therapeutic support did not materialise. The most common causes of disruption are incomplete information, inaccurate assessments of trauma and loss and inadequate resources. We may have to stand by while seemingly promising placements crumble, but more often we can watch in respectful admiration as children and parents, with incalculable effort and patience, make the most improbable placements for adoption last.

If disruption becomes inevitable, it will be painful for all concerned, and that includes the relatives by adoption. Anger, guilt, resentment, shame and bewilderment are the feelings on the surface, and depression lurks beneath.

My daughter and son-in-law adopted a little boy aged five, a year ago. He was very difficult to manage but I loved him like my own grandchild and I think he loved me. He didn't ever settle down and my daughter couldn't take it any more. He used to hit her and spit at her and shout that she wasn't his real mummy. He was better with my son-in-law and in school and he was always better

---

with me but that only made it worse. She had all
the help there was and she tried everything they
said, but nothing worked. He was taken away by
social services. I know he's been placed with
another family but I don't know where. I can't
speak to my daughter about it because she just
clams up or bursts out crying. I feel I've lost my
only grandson and he's lost me. How could they
do it?
Grandparent after disruption

When a placement is beyond help, adopters may have to give up
for the child's sake as well as their own. The only way to make
disruption less traumatic at the end is to manage it as carefully as
the introductions at the beginning. The child and family (including
the grandmother above) need an intensive period of preparation for
disruption, as well as support to maintain contact and continuity
after the child has moved. If the adopters have been badly wounded
and fear that they have damaged the child, they may want to cut
off completely. If grandparents and other relatives, who may
themselves be hurting, can show sympathy and understanding
for the parents, a cut-off may be avoided.

09

A tale of two generations of grandparents

This photo shows some members of our family when we got together at Christmas. When we started our large mixed family group, fortunately both sets of grandparents-to-be went along with our plans.

Grandparents have always been important in our family. It is a family that has the long memory that emerges from mining communities in which elders are seen as vital links in transmitting culture to the new generations. As children, of course, we would not have put it like that. It was just obvious that grandparents are the tellers of enthralling stories and the providers of juicy information about the world before we were born – especially the information about their own early lives that would embarrass our parents and delight us. They were also the living images of stages in our own genetic inheritance, indicators of what life held in store for us. Grandparents were our history and our future.

When we started our large mixed family group, we were very concerned to continue that tradition. Fortunately both sets of grandparents-to-be went along with our plans, and, whatever their private concerns or anxieties, agreed to share in the adventure of enlarging the family.

Being a grandparent in an enlarged family group
Joyce and Eric Stanway

We remember with crystal clarity the day our daughter and son-in-law told us that they were planning to join the Children's Family Trust (CFT) and take on a ready made family of assorted foster children. Not too bad, we thought, since we knew that foster placements were always provisional, frequently broke down, and that if children were difficult they could, and indeed would, be taken away and placed elsewhere. This was, we believed, a necessary and essential service designed to settle children down after traumas and difficulties at home or school as part of their general preparation for a life of independence. And then we read the principles underlying CFT, and it became clear that for CFT fostering was essentially adoption. It was axiomatic to the Trust that a child entering a CFT family was being offered a family for life.

Our backgrounds should have made it easier for us to accept the family changes. We already had considerable experience of working with children from broken homes or who were posing problems at school. Eric was headmaster and Joyce was matron and head of care at a local authority residential school for children with special needs. In those days they were officially classified as "maladjusted" though it was not a term we used in our normal dealings with children and families. We soon discovered that our role as instant grandparents was to be quite different. Pitched in at the deep end, we found ourselves having to adjust very rapidly to a new way of life. Suddenly we acquired a whole new set of relationships and responsibilities.

Few days passed without some contact with this new generation of our family, across the whole range from babysitting to give the new parents some time out, through to children just dropping in on their way home from school. It was clear that we were providing some important anchor points for the children. We could give them vital information about these mysterious people who they were struggling to identify as new parents. Delicate (and indelicate) questions were endless. We were also a way for the child to understand more about the family they had joined. We watched them watching us and trying to learn how this family ticked.

Joyce had one built in advantage. She was not just a good cook, but she had the inestimable gift of producing food, which was instantly attractive to youngsters. Granny's Glup, for instance, as it was named by an articulate eight-year-old, was a kind of fruit jelly and trifle laced with chocolate drops. It was one of those 'Granny made it specially for us' things of which the children never seemed to tire. Eric exercised his talent for story telling at bedtime, weaving the children's names and background histories into a series of fantastic jungle and treasure island adventures. The children would remember every detail of the story so far, and gradually became much freer in adding to the story themselves.

A couple of cameos illustrate our involvement with the children and the development of the essential relationships, which underpin "normal" family life. In 1976 – remember the year of the great drought? – to allow Kate and Brian time with their newborn baby just home from hospital, we took six children on holiday for a week to Butlin's at Minehead. When we were arranging the holiday, we were asked the ages of the children – ten, nine, eight, seven, six, and four – and were told, 'Well, sir, you'll need two chalets'. 'That's all right. Our 22-year-old daughter will come with us to look after the second chalet.' What we did not think about was that the staff at Butlin's assumed that these were all our own children, and were waiting with some eager curiosity to see this fecund family disembark from the minibus.

For the record, the holiday was an unqualified success. The chain link fence around the camp and the gatekeepers on duty may be the cause of many jokes about Stalag 22, but they give remarkable peace of mind to anxious grandparents. The relaxed atmosphere, the excellent programmes for all ages, and the general air of family harmony, made time flash past. A small baby undoubtedly needs to be in the arms of parents, but for these older children, whose own parents were not available, grandparents could be an unthreatening way to finding love and care.

A second occasion may illustrate the way in which we, as grandparents, felt we could provide the opportunity for the children to express their growing trust and pride in their new family. Summer evenings were often perfect for family barbecues, usually impromptu affairs involving just whoever happened to be around at the time and whatever food we could find at short notice. At one such event, one of the grandchildren turned up with 20 or so French schoolchildren and their exchange hosts in tow. 'We knew it would be all right. Our Gran is used to coping with big numbers.' God bless the little darlings!

So where does it end? The short answer is that it doesn't. The youngest of the 15 is now 24 and they have all left home, but they keep in touch and at times of family crisis there is always mutual support at all levels. Then there are the many occasions when family members gather together. Special birthdays, like a recent eightieth, weddings, funerals, and christenings are all the stuff out of which the family stories are made and will continue to grow into the next generation. From time to time, family holidays are arranged, and as the group grows with the addition of partners and children and stepchildren, so the venues become progressively more of a challenge. Last time we took a whole chateau, enough gîtes to accommodate all the separate family units. Next time it will be a wedding in Greece, and the apartment block has been booked well in advance.

So the grandparents are now great-grandparents many times over. Looking back, there have been laughter, tears, some heartache, but overwhelmingly joy in the happy realisation that a disparate group of unhappy and wounded youngsters has become a family unit.

The next generation
Kate Cairns

Thirty years ago when we started our large family the world was very different. Most children lived in two parent families and the parents were a man and woman married to each other. Now our society is diverse, and childhood occurs in a different environment and with quite different sets of assumptions. When our parents became grandparents to our mixed group of children, they had to open themselves to a previously unimaginable journey of discovery before they could establish what being grandparents to these children could be. Fortunately for us they were willing and able to make that journey, and with a sufficient measure of evident delight in the process to reassure us that we had not blighted their lives. The expression they give to the experience makes it clear that they feel that they have gained and grown because of it.

When I try to think about being a grandparent to the next generation, however, I realise fully the impact of the changes we have all seen in those 30 years. Our constituted family is no longer such an oddity among so many reconstituted ones. Our children have a fair track record for stability of relationships, but like most grandparents now, we have had to learn how to relate to divorce, remarriage, and half- and step-relationships. We have, beyond question, had to learn new ways of relating to the families our children have formed. But I have discovered that every issue for us has also been an issue for other grandparents, who have started from a more conventional family structure as a base. In many ways our unconventional family has been an excellent preparation for the rapid learning almost all grandparents now have to do.

We have also been subject to all the other effects of the demographic changes that have reshaped our society over the last 30 years. We are now the middle generation of five generations, with ages ranging from 1 to 95. The generations above us are as likely to need our thought and care as those below. We are also, by necessity, both in full-time employment. Our grandchildren, though much loved, cannot have first call on our time. Fortunately, most of our children who have children have had the foresight to have partners whose own parents are less encumbered. We can be second-string grandparents without a qualm.

It is clear that we are inventing ourselves as grandparents as we go along. Yet without conscious intent, the key features of being a grandparent in our family, re-emerge. We are the holders of memory, the tellers of stories, and the embodiments of continuity and succession for our grandchildren. Each of the children is different, yet we observe that for each one there is an element in their making sense of the world that includes us. We create opportunities for family occasions and celebrations, and are there as a steady presence in an uncertain world. We can be both more indulgent and more old fashioned than we were as their parents. I do have a mobile phone, but I don't understand text messaging ("bless!" is a constant text interjection from one grandchild as she attempts to bring me up to date with technology). I do like music, but have no idea who or what Eminem might be.

We can answer questions about what their parents were like as children. And we can remind parents gently at points of dispute with their children that it is just possible that the emergence of wilfulness or temper in a child often looks remarkably similar to the patterns in the previous generation, and that children take after their parents in more than just appearance. We can also be the arbitrators and advisers in a whole range of family difficulties if those tasks are laid upon us, though it is always the most delicate of negotiations to be involved in the family life of the next generation.

I remember being told when I was a child that I was exactly like my Auntie Lizzie Rutter, a formidable character who was the village midwife and layer-out of the dead. At the time I thought it nonsense. Apart from anything else, she was old, and therefore utterly unlike me. She was also, intriguingly, no relative at all. In that mining village she was simply the universal ancestor, a person who would reappear in every generation. Now that I am as old as Lizzie Rutter was then, I find that I am, to some extent, becoming my ancestors. A constant delight in the continuing development of our family is to observe the extent to which each of the fostered children has added that ancestry to their own unique history.

Our parents, like most of their generation, had a clear sense of what it meant to be a grandparent, such relationships being fixed by history and precedent. They had to embrace a radical change in their expectations and assumptions in order to become grandparents to the family we formed. By contrast, we find ourselves in much the same position as many of our friends, having to invent what it means to be a grandparent in the twenty-first century in Britain.

10

Endpiece:
What you can do

She was our first grandchild. We didn't know anything about adoption, we didn't know what was expected of us or what we could manage. It was like taking a leap into the unknown – but it was worth it.
Parents of adopters

What do you want to do? What do you think you should do? What can you do?

Not every grandparent, aunt, uncle or cousin will want to be involved if someone in the family plans to adopt. All relations, including grandparents, will have their own life to lead and the family style may be to remain related at a distance, whether children are born into the family or adopted. Before making a commitment to support the prospective adopters, it is wise to ask yourself: 'What do I want to do?' Do you want to be actively involved wherever possible? Or do you want to be included only if needed and say what you think only if asked? Do you want to offer regular help with child care or just occasional babysitting? Do you want to be indispensable or merely available?

Don't let yourself be too much influenced by what you think you should do. Having children by adoption, like having children by birth, has to be the responsibility of the parents. It may be lovely if the family is the kind of family that rallies round, but not all families do, and some parents may prefer it if they don't. There is no reason why you should respond to an adoption in the family in any other way than to a birth. If you find it difficult to respond in the same way, because the child is not related to you, then give yourself time. It's no help trying to tell yourself how you ought to feel, if you don't. It's a good enough start to treat an adopted child with the respect, kindness and consideration you would normally show to anyone who came to stay with your family.

What you want to do and what you think you should do may not be quite the same as what you can do. You may be asking too much of yourself; there may be family conflicts, which get in the way; distances between family members may be too daunting; or you may simply have to earn a living. It is important not to raise expectations of help and support too high, before a child arrives, if there is a danger of having to let adopters and children down later.

*I wish now that I'd not promised to look after him
in the mornings while my daughter works. I hadn't
looked after a little one for so long and he was all
over the place and it wore me out. I had to tell her
– it caused a lot of bad feeling. She's still upset
with me and Social Services blame her for not
sorting it out beforehand and I blame myself
because the little one's been put in a nursery now
and he doesn't like it.*
Mother of single adopter

Better to restrict yourself, from the beginning, to what you know
you can manage. It is easier then for adopters to make
arrangements for the support they will need. And reading to a child,
each time you visit, can be as rewarding for both of you as daily
childcare. One eight-year-old wrote in class: *'when grandparents
read to us they don't skip and they don't mind if we ask for the
same story again'.*

Stories have made many appearances in this brief book. There are
the stories children bring into new families and the stories families
have to tell. These are the stories that get woven together into the
adoption story. And the adoption story grows and, like all good
stories, gets handed down from one generation to the next. Stories
are the stuff of life; they bear witness to the continuity of people
and of communities. Everyone has their very own story and adds
layers to the stories of others. Relatives by adoption have a
contribution to make to the adoption story and their own stories
will become enriched by the adoption experience. Adopted children,
like all children, love to have relations. As another eight-year-old in
the same class wrote:

*Everybody should try to have a grandmother or grandfather
or aunt or uncle, especially if they don't have television,
because they are the only grown-ups who have spare time to
spend with us.*

Useful organisations

ADOPTION UK
A UK-wide self-help group supporting adoptive families before, during and after adoption.
Linden House
55 The Green
South Bar Street
Banbury
Oxfordshire OX16 9AB
Tel: 01295 752240
www.adoptionuk.org.uk

BRITISH ASSOCIATION FOR ADOPTION AND FOSTERING (BAAF)
A UK-wide organisation for everyone who works in adoption, fostering and childcare.
Saffron House
6–10 Kirby Street
London EC1N 8TS
Tel: 020 7421 2600
www.baaf.org.uk

FAMILY RIGHTS GROUP (FRG)
A national organisation that advises on family law and childcare practice.
The Print House
18 Ashwin Street
London E8 3DL
Advice line: 0808 801 0366
www.frg.org.uk

GRANDPARENTS' ASSOCIATION
A self-help group supporting grandparents.
Moot House
The Stow
Harlow
Essex CM20 3AG
Helpline: 0845 434 9585
www.grandparents-association.org.uk

GRANDPARENTS PLUS
A national organisation that offers consultation and training for grandparents, plus other relatives and professionals.
18 Victoria Park Square
Bethnal Green
London E2 9PF
Tel: 020 8981 8001
www.grandparentsplus.org.uk

Suggestions for further reading

Argent H (1998) *Whatever Happened to Adam?*, London: BAAF
A collection of stories of disabled young people and the families who chose to care for them.

Argent H (ed) (2002) *Staying Connected*, London: BAAF
An anthology of papers which look at ways of managing contact arrangements in adoption.

Cairns K (2002) *Attachment, Trauma and Resilience*, London: BAAF
A beautifully written account of a personal and professional experience of living with children who have been hurt.

Lord J (2010) *Adopting a Child*, London: BAAF
A popular guide to adoption and how to go about it.

Salter A (2011) *The Adopter's Handbook*, London: BAAF
Information, resources and services for adoptive families.

Thomas C and Beckford V (1999) *Adopted Children Speaking*, London: BAAF
A poignant and moving record of children's wishes and feelings about adoption and their experience of it.

To order any of these books, and to see details of many more adoption and fostering titles, visit www.baaf.org.uk.